Hearty Vehemence Vol I

The collection of poems straight from my heart

Navneet Agarwal

pencil

ISBN 978-93-5610-882-0

Published in India 2022 by Pencil

A brand of
One Point Six Technologies Pvt. Ltd.
123, Building J2, Shram Seva Premises,
Wadala Truck Terminal, Wadala (E)
Mumbai 400037, Maharashtra, INDIA
E connect@thepencilapp.com
W www.thepencilapp.com

Author biography

Being Born in 1991 in the small hilly town of Darjeeling, I did my schooling from the St. Joseph's College, School Department, commonly called North Point. Thereafter I went to Delhi and did my graduation from Dyal Singh College, University of Delhi. First I taught Mathematics in the Assembly of God Church School, and there after I went to Delhi and worked as a maths expert for NCR Eduservices. This made me rethink and I did my masters in Economics from IGNOU and then B.Ed from CRSU. I currently work with the Assembly of God Church School as their Economics Teacher.

I have had the passion for writing since a long time, and started to write poems after my mother's death. I have written few books as well.

CONTENTS

Sorrow..7

Pain of My Heart..8

Missing You...10

Survival Strategy..13

Difference in Behaviour...14

Life...16

Life Trouble..18

My Regret...21

Promises...23

Life Choices..25

Monsoon...27

Life's Chapter..29

I Miss You...30

Time Is Precious..32

I want to Sleep...33

Why do People Underestimate...35

Alone in Relationships...36

Mistakes..38

Mother...40

Things in Heart..41

Winter Coming..43

Speak Carefully 45
News Good or Bad 47
My Thought 49
Love 51
Nature Difference 53
Confusion 54
Lost in Thought 56
Corruption Vs Communalism 58
Trust Issue 60
HOLI 62
Jealousy 64
Farewell 66
Mother's Day 68
Mistakes I have made... 70
Confession 72
Do I have Friends 74
My Love 76
Child Within 78
You will be Remembered 80
Rain Dance 82
Fate and Luck 83
Mother- a precious gift 85
Dreams 87
Responsibility 89

Letter to Mom 91

Truth 93

Superstition 95

Sorrow

Today is the day of sorrow for me
I should be happy I know, but, I am missing you
You were my life, you were everything to me
The only thing that I miss is you

In this life I cannot forget you
You were the life support system for me
Without you I am a life less zombie
Your words gave life like powers to me

My life can never be complete without you
You are that part which completes me
I was never able to express my feelings
That's the only regret that haunts me

Why did you leave me in such a misery
In such a state of despair
I never thought that fate will play such a game with me
And take you away from me and leave me without a pair

Pain of My Heart

Words pain more than actions
But it is not always
You may pour your heart out
But it doesn't relief you always

You need to have a control
On your tongue
If you don't, you live old
But actually you die young

Always think before
You open your mouth
But if you don't
It will turn as your gout

Relationships break
You build up frenemies
And they are worse
Even worse than enemies

It's anger which I have controlled
Now for ages
The outburst happens
In the difficulty of voyages

I kept quiet then
As I knew it was required of me
Now I have become completely silent
As now I had to be

How much can someone bare?
How much can someone care?
I have lost my patience now
And what shall happen I don't care

I knew they were like that
But I had no other option
I tried to maintain it
But now they left me no option

I miss you mom
But still feel it's better you are gone
I never wanted to come back
But I had to for the reason that was not done

I have stepped in your shoes
To do the work as you would
Now I had to do it
Which much before I should

The mission has begun
The missiles are launched
It will take time now
As the pain is totally haunched

Missing You

I am in a dilemma today
As I have nothing to say
The things are not
At all going in my way

I was of the opinion
That I just would be happy
But without you
The jokes also make me unhappy

I learnt many things
And all goes to your credit
The things which you taught me
Always make my life debit

I receive love
Wherever I go
It just looks like sympathy
But why I don't know

Your teachings
Have made my life comfortable
But you are not there with me
To take your advice and make it applaud able

I love you so much
But I never did tell you
Now I know it is too late
I wish I could tell you

I had only one asset
And that was only you
I have always been your liability
And now I cannot repay you

I wish you could
Give me advice like you did before
But you are no more with me
And so I have no one to help therefore

You enlightened me
And always gave me hope
You showed me directions
And gave me a strong scope

I always wanted
To nourish you like you did to me
But God wanted you more
And so he made you and me never see

You have gone far far away
And it's beyond my reach
I always feel you around me
And my heart is our meeting beach

I love you
And I always did

I never showed you
Which I never did!!!

Survival Strategy

You sometimes have to be very harsh
But sometimes as soft as a flower
Sometimes you have to be cruel enough
And sometimes like the smell of a flower
When things are not according to your way
You have to fight through it
When you are in danger
You have to protect it

The world is not like you
It is very cruel
You have to struggle through
And use the smart sewel

It's not that easy to survive
If you take everyone in the same way
Everyone is different
And you have to befriend anyone in the stay

There is no other way to survive
Love can always not change the way
Neither hate nor jealousy can
You have to be on the train anyway.

Difference in Behaviour

The whole thing comes
As a surprise to me
How do people behave
Differently to the different people they see

It may be
In the human nature
To behave that way
But still they do it in the future

I am also
Not an exception to it
The rule applies to me also
But still I am inquisitive about it

I love the way
People change their tone
It's psychological
And I am also not left alone

Everyone
Has a hidden face
The face which can't be seen
And if you find it, it's spade of ace

According to me
You have to hide that face
You have to make it your strength
And then you win the heart of ace

Whether you agree or not
You also are the part of the league
You may try to deny the fact
But you are like any other fish

But still I wonder
Why is it the only way?
Why do we have to behave
In such a different way?

Life

Today is the day
When I have nothing else to say
But I can see that
It has been done in the wrong way

Why do such things happen?
Why are we put in such a situation?
Why does such a time come?
When we don't have a solution.

People tend to forget
What were their actions
And then act per their wish
In any situation

It's difficult to understand
The mentality of people
We may think something else
And that may create a problem

The allegations you get
Are may be for your betterment
You have to cherish it
And change your thought sequence

In your life
Everyone can't love you
The hate from someone
Is actually what changes you

Life Trouble

How much to handle?
How much could be beared?
It has become so difficult
And I want to be spared

It's an everyday scene
It's a normal routine
The things have now crossed its limits
I wish I could be set free

I have right now nowhere to go
I am stuck in an unbound circle
It's the promise that keeps me
From breaking this vicious circle

I always hated the mundane things
I always wanted something new
It's been a lot of time now
That I have done something new

I force myself
To work for him
I am bound by the promise
To take care of him

I am in a big dilemma
Why did God do this to me?
What sins I had done
That he took away my mom from me?

I always shared
All my problems with her
Now it's very difficult for me
To find a replacement for her

Why do some people
Take others for granted
Only think about oneself
And think nobody is wanted

Mistakes are made
That ruin the life
They are such mistakes maybe
Which take you away from your true life

Why do even after growing old
Some people are worse than kids
They are childish every time
But never look like they have sinned

I never wanted to grow up
But responsibilities made me do so
When the elders are just like children
You have no other choice for

I miss my mom so much
She has always been my idol

Her way of living inspires me
Her words were ideal

She taught me to handle everything
To face all the situation
Her teachings make me live
She has made me a true human being

My Regret

I wanted to give you all the happiness
But why when I can give you, you are not there with me
I want to go back in time
And stop you from making the decision to leave me

I am in a situation now
Where there is no way
I didn't want you to part from me
In such an untold way

I know whatever happens
Always happens for a hidden good
But the time and moment
Is not allowing me to find that good

I know you are in a better place
Better than what you have been
Heaven is the only place you deserve
But I wanted to make your life heaven that is not seen

I don't regret you leaving me
As you have always nurtured me
But the thought of not giving you what you deserved
Is that everyday which kills me

I loved only you
No one else can ever take that place
I know that it is weird
But nobody, how much they try, can never fill that space.

I had never thought
That you will leave me so fast
Me never fulfilling your dreams
Is the only saddest part

I always cry
But not near anyone
I will always miss you
But I know you will never return as now you have gone

I used to share, everything with you
Till now I haven't found that worthy trust
I fear in showing my inner thoughts and feelings
As now I fear to burden anyone like I had burdened you first.

Promises

Promise is the word
You need to break it
But why is it not possible
For me to break it?

I promised my mom
To take care of my dad
Though it is difficult for me to do so
But I can never make her sad

I even promised her
To give a good life to my sis
I tried my best to do so
But I always have a human miss

I promised my sister
To take care of my brother
I have been doing it unconditionally
And he will have me always there

I promised the lord
That I will never ask him any favour
I have lived up to it
And have never begged him of a favour

I promised my friends
To always remember them
But now it seems to me
I am only trying to do the same

I promised myself
Never to break any of my promises
I have been trying to do so
And have kept all of my promises

Life Choices

There is one thing
Which I have in my mind
This thing of mine
Is not bound by time

Be careful in making choices
Be careful in choosing your way
Be careful in taking sides
Be careful of what you say

In a dilemma
Always think twice
See all the pros and cons
And then do a wise choice

In your life
Take the road which you want to
Always listen to everyone's advice
And then do that you have to

In a fight
Never take anyone's side
Try to reunite the fighters
And that is considered wise

The word which once come out
Cannot be taken back
If you don't think and speak
It may give your life a wack

Monsoon

Monsoon is a special season
Unlike the other ones
It has necessary evil reasons
Which are very important ones

Economically,
It boosts the fertility of land
But sometimes
It brings flood in that same land

Romance
Is in the air when it rains
But if you see
The house of Poor goes in drains

Biologically,
It hydrates all the living things
But it also
Sickens some human beings

Environmentally,
It provides water to the forest
But it also
Causes landslides uprooting the forest

It is on you
To take it in which way
It is
The life in an actual say

Life's Chapter

The whole world in actuality is a myth
It's very hard for anyone to believe
It's actually not very simple understanding
But as time comes you have to believe

There is always an end to every chapter
And it is very obvious to say
The end sometimes id very happy
But that in actuality is very difficult to say

You just miss those
Whom you love the most
But the end is just a beginning
For a new chapter which has things lost

You never know when your chapter ends
Just the chapter needs to be memorable
No matter how many twists and turns it has
It needs to be adorable

I Miss You

The whole world is empty
There is no place to go
In my times of despair
I really miss you

I shared everything with you
I loved you with my full heart
I just wanted to sacrifice myself for you
If I was given a chance

It's not possible to forget you
In no way can I replace you
You will always be there in my memory
I can see you in your photo only

I just can't say anything
In no way can I describe you
The whole thing is simple
It's very difficult for me to live without you

I thought I will be there for you
But God didn't want this to happen
He took you away from me
And just made my life sadden

I miss you mom so much
It's very difficult for me to tell
I never thought you will leave me
And let my life sail

Time Is Precious

Every time it's the time which place with you
Your desires your emotions your everything
It's not that it always teaches you good
Sometimes for your own benefit or something

It's not just the passing away that reminds you of it
When it's still there you hardly consider it
It is there with you always
What it is very difficult to recognise it

It is said that time is precious
But it has no actual value
Time is sometimes worthless
And after that we see its value

People say do not waste it
But what to do if you have nothing to do
People say utilise it properly
But sometimes there is no work to do.

I want to Sleep

Now I am tired, now I want to sleep
I want a holiday and that's from everything
I want a day off from the mundane routine
I want to just sleep for the whole day indeed

I don't want to wake up, get out of bed
I don't want to receive calls when I sleep
I don't want WhatsApp and hike for a day
I just want to change my status to just sleep

I want to be out of Facebook during the sleep
I want to be not included anywhere in anything
I don't want the doorbell to ring
I don't want anyone to disturb me for anything

I will call it the sleep day and call it off
I want to be away it seems as I had enough
I just want to sleep and get lost In My Dreams
I want to even dream of sleep if it is not enough

I want no one to wake me up
I want to be dead for that day
Away from Social Network
And not seen by anyone during that day

I know it's not possible for me to do that
As I have stepped in someone's shoes which don't befit
I knew it will never be easy anytime
As I was acquainted with the difficulty in it

Why do People Underestimate

Why do people underestimate?
Why do they think they are not able?
What makes them feel inferior?
Why do they think they are incapable?

Everyone has their own capabilities
Why feel inferior for that?
Everyone has a different way of thinking
Why feel incapable of that?

The lifestyle may be different
Why feel you cannot adjust?
The way of showing love may be different
Why feel your way is not just?
You may be low in somethings
Why make it a great one?
People may even judge you
Why think that you are the left one?
The whole world will be after you
If you think in such a manner
You need to show only one thing
That you are an opportunity taker.

Alone in Relationships

I can't stop crying today
My heart is full of sorrow
All my happiness it seems
Are hidden in a burrow

It seems I am alone
No one is there for me
The whole world is there
Just to mock me

I thought the doings of life
Are always reciprocated
But now it feels
Helping others is rather a mistake

You come alone to this world
You will go alone
The relations you bind yourself with
Are just temporary throne

No one helps you
When the tide is low
During the high tide
There are a lots of faces which show

It seems absurd
To think in such a way
But as the time comes
You will be left with no say

You love your family
Which may not be always there
You have hopes from your family
Which is always a despair

Mistakes

Mistakes are a part of life
They help you grow up
It is essential to make a mistake
To reach to the top

Nobody can be perfect
No one can actually win
Without a mistake done
And then never repeated it

Mistakes if repeated
Can be termed as a novice
If done more then twice
It can be said to be a crime

You need to
Make a habit
To make a mistake
And then learn to never repeat it.

You have to be careful
Not to repeat it
You have to learn
The basics from it

Mistakes are a part of life
If you don't make it you are God
If you are a human
Accept it you will not feel odd

Always accept your mistakes
It will help you improve
But if you don't
It may so happen that your relations deprove

Mother

Mother is the God's face on Earth
As he can't be with you everywhere
He created Mother
To be with you anytime anywhere

She does the chores
Without any complaints
She does all the work
Without any alliance

Her life is dedicated
To her child and her family
Whatever she thinks or does
Is only for her family

Things in Heart

When you have a lot of things
In your heart
And you are not sure when to
Tell a part

You know your emotions
Will be made fun of
You may trust them with the secret
But the whole thing is made tough

You come to this world alone
You will leave alone
You need to learn to live
In this condition all along

Your plans may not work
Your dreams will shatter
You will be left alone
And for everyone leave a chance for laughter

The thought process is hidden
You are mesmerised with your forgone plan
You are in a trouble now
And you have to be in alarm

The whole world is dark now
The lights have gone
You don't see anyone now
Everyone is gone

In such a situation
You don't see the spark of light
Your hopes are in dungeons
And now you have to sit tight

Winter Coming

The cold weather
The chilly morning
The frozen wind
That's winter coming

The chimney smoke
The burning wooden things
The bourne-fire games
That's winter coming

The cold water
The dew during the morning
The frost on the roof
That's winter coming

You don't want to
Leave your bed
Do all the work
Without getting out of bed

The hot water bottles
The switched on heaters
The slices of orange
The old and lovely sweaters

Winter is amazing
It is one of its kind
I love the season
It's my favourite and is always mine

Speak Carefully

Always be careful
Of what you speak
Think twice and choose the words
Proper care has to be taken in this

You just can't say
What comes out of you
It may sometimes be hurtful
And go against you

All the feelings of your heart
Can't be poured out
Some has to be buried deeply
So that it is never found out

Speak less
If you think you can't control
Don't talk when you are low
Otherwise others will take hold

It is not easy to burden
Your heart this way
But it's better to be silent
Than to say and later pay

It may seem
That you have said to a friend
But sometimes it is not good
To share everything with a friend

When things change
You will not know
When friends become enemy
You will not know

So it is better
Not to say all the things
And if you do speak
You need to have wings

News Good or Bad

Everyday you get news
Good or bad it may be
Everyone gives you a news
Happy or sad it may be

Today I was burdened
With news of mixed feeling
I don't have words for it
And my heart is beating

The news was not
Actually a surprise for me
I knew the arrival of it
At the news was supported by me

But the delivery of the news
Came as a shock
For a while I felt like
I have turned into a rock

I was lost in the thought
Of never seeing someone in future
I was still happy being sad
As he did it for his better

This was not only
The news which I received today
There was one more
And that mesmerised me today

I had never thought
I was loved to that extent
I feel happy that I have made a good friend
And I shall never repent

There was one more news
But it was what happens
It is life that we need to accept
It always salute the things that happens

I don't know any other way
To express myself
I will never forget my dear ones
Even if I forget myself

My Thought

I am trapped in my thoughts
My thought is very weird
I simply can't express it
It's really very geared

I want to run away
From every situation
From the anxious heart
From all the creation

I know I don't have an option
I have to stay back
Why can't I simply love him
And for see what he lacks

I am not selfish
But can't control my desires
I love myself very much
But have to kill my desires

I had never dreamt of such a life
I have to be happy with it
I feel very helpless sometimes
But have to live with it

Yes, you may say
That I always think negatively
But actually I have no other way
To express my feelings so easily

I have not seen the world much
Neither have not seen it at all
I am sly I know
But that is what I had been taught

Love

Life has a lot of trouble
You need to face it
When you don't have any idea
Love is the thing that rescues you of it

Love is not limited to
A girl and a boy
It's scope is very wide
You can even love a toy

When you open your eyes
Your mother was your first love
She defines love for you
But soon you forget her love

You soon find your siblings
And also your cousins
They are your first friend
Their love is later thrown into the Dungeons

As you grow up
There are friends who occupy your heart
They become your fixed deposits
And they are your love life's part

When a woman comes in your life
She becomes the important thing
You need her for eternity
And you don't consider any other thing

Don't mistake the love with
The act of love making
It's not just the lust which is there
Love is actually in every relationship building

So dear friend of mine
You love your family and friends
It may not be told
But love should be shown in your actions

Love is a wonderful gift
Which is the grave part of your life
You love everyone around you
All these people make a mark in your life

But there is one important thing
You need to always love yourself
As, if you don't do it
You will never be able to enjoy yourself

Never underestimate yourself
Others are there for that
Love yourself like you are your girlfriend
And always gives your back yourself a pat

Nature Difference

I just don't know
What is happening?
I am getting angry
Upon very little things

It's not very usual
It's very different for me
I have really experienced
It's a new thing that I see

I don't know what it is
It's a very new character for me
I think I am getting crazy
But it's like a new thing you see

Confusion

When you are alone you think a lot
All bad thoughts come to you
You take small things seriously
That makes a fool of you

I think a lot when I am alone
It makes me angry sometimes
But anxiety does not last much
And it cools me down sometimes

This time all the thoughts that come
Are only making me worse
At a time I feel like to cry
The only time I want to crush

I am so lost right now
I feel that I made some wrong decisions
I don't know why I feel so
But then justify those decisions

I am so confused right now
Were the things I have chosen right
I don't know what is wrong in them
There is going on an inner fight

I need to find the way out
I actually need some guidance
The answers are I know within me
I just need some evidence

Lost in Thought

I am lost in my thoughts
Thinking what is going wrong
Why am I stuck in one place?
Why do I have to be in the same song?

I tried to change my location
But it is not working
I have to do something to improve
But I am not getting anything

I have done mistakes in my life
Which cannot be undone
I have understood one thing
Grab the opportunities before they are gone

I think too much before doing anything
And that is a big problem
I think playing this is not the main thing
You need to take risk and build your emblem

The great people always took risk
That's why they are great
Then why am I afraid to take risk
Maybe I think too much to be great

I was never inspired
By The Thinker
But still I think too much
And that's my sinker

I am lost in my own self
The thought of it is weirder
I simply don't have much choices
And that makes it sadder

I need some inspiration
Someone to motivate me
I think I am throwing My Life Away
I need someone to guide me

Corruption Vs Communalism

The main problem in India
Is not corruption
You may hardly believe me
But it's actually communalism

Corruption is a problem
I don't deny that fact at all
But communism is no less a problem
As you see the things involved

What is communalism?
Is the question that now arise
The answer is there within the word
but no one wants to against it Fight

Inter-caste marriage is not allowed
Inter-religion is also there involved
Love Jihad is the new word invented
And also the difference involved

You may prove me wrong
You may say corruption is still big
As we don't think the other way round
As everyone is stuck to this

All political leaders
Try to win the elections on the communal grounds
The promise to fight corruption
But after winning, talk communal the year round

So the discretion is yours
It's for you to decide
Which is a bigger problem
With corruption and communalism on either side

Trust Issue

Don't trust everyone for everything
Never make this mistake
You don't know anything about them
This may put your life at stake

What you say to others
May be used against you someday
You will never know what has happened
But you will repent everyday

You may think that they are your friends
The best buddies indeed
They are actually what we say
The wolves in the sheep's skin

They come close to you
So that you can trust them
They then show their true colours
And still you are unaware of them

You still trust them
With all your heart
You trust them blindly
And tell them every part

They use it against you
In order to make their progress
You need to be careful
As you are the one to loose in that case

When you come to know the truth
You may still not believe it
You are not devastated in your thoughts
And it makes it hard and you sit

You don't want to trust anyone again
You are no more in your senses
It takes time for you to regain
And then come back to senses

It's an advice for you to take
Don't believe on anyone
Think twice before you speak
Don't say every secret to everyone

HOLI

Holi it seems to be
A festival of colours indeed
It's the time when
We colour our sorrows indeed

All the colours
Represent different things
The all denote
The different song you sing

It's the time
When you mingle with friends
You forget the things of past
And surpass every means

The faces smeared in colours
The joy hidden everywhere
The scent of the sweets
Are coming from everywhere

It is said as a time of love
The time which brings you closer
The time which makes you
Love your partner for ever

But there is another side
Some evils have crept into it
Some people tend to cross their limits
And do some illegal things during it

They take everything for granted
They consider everyone is made for them
They take every opportunity
To make evil love to people around them

It is a sad reality
But nothing can be done
We can only take pledges ourselves
That we won't mix lust in holi and everything is itself done

Jealousy

Why do people get jealous
On others' success?
Why can't they live their own life
And mind their own business?

I just don't understand
Why are people like that?
They have problems in all
The success you have

They make plans
To ruin your work
They do anything and everything
To ruin your effort

You may be good
At what you do
But these things are for real
Will always affect you

You might think that
Why are they acting in such a way
You haven't said anything against them
You haven't got in there way

But still they will
Obstruct your path
They will do whatever they can
To make you give up at last

You should not give up
You should show them
They have messed with a wrong person
And just do your work near them

Jealousy means
You are good enough
As, if you are not
They would not have done that

Be happy that
You have jealous people around you
They will actually make you grow
Indirectly they are working for you

Farewell

On my first day
I didn't know that he will be a guiding light for me
But since my two years
He has been a father figure for me

He always has a game plan
He always motivated me
He has been a true mentor
And the real guardian for me

I took him as a father itself
I will always cherish what he taught me
He has always been a pillar
And his teachings will never be forgotten by me

It was my luck
To have him there always
And I was inspired by him
To be there for him always

The news came to me
As a very big shock
It threw me speechless
And I was unable to recover from that

It broke my heart
I was shattered into pieces
He deserved a proper farewell
Not the way it has been done

I loved him
And the feeling of respect will always come
I hope he stays happy
And prosper in the years to come

Mother's Day

Today is Mother's day
The day when you appreciate your mother
It's a very special day
The actual God is your mother

I don't want to be sad
I want to be happy today
It's been two years now
You left me and have gone away

No one can fill your space
No one is as worthy as you have been
You were my best friend
Such a worthy friend indeed

I know in no way can
This message be conveyed to you
You are in such a place
Where I can hope happiness for you

If there is any possibility
I want to have a partner like you
I will be lucky enough
If I fall in love with a person as worthy as you.

If there is life after death
The concept of rebirth exists
I would like to have you again
As my mother if it possibly exists

I love you Mom
I will always do
I hope you are watching me
And being proud of what I will do

I wanted to share
A lot of things with you
But what to do
God wanted only one thing and that is you

I do talk to your photograph
Though they are few
But the only problem with them is
That they don't give advices like you

Mistakes I have made...

We humans have a nature
To ignore our mistakes
We overlook the faults in us
And happened to mock others mistake

I have made a lot of mistakes
I know
I am not a perfect human being
And this fact I know

I cannot show my love
In true sense
I cannot say I love you
In any case

I have a problem
I cannot appreciate others
But that doesn't mean
I don't want it from others

I have made a mistake
Of not accepting my mistake
I can never do it
I have never learnt to be fake

Whatever you do for me
I tend to forget
Whatever bad you say to me
I will never forget

I just believe in monetary benefits
I say money is bigger than love
According to me you can buy anything with money
Money can even buy love

I am admitting my flaws
And I know that is also a mistake
If I would not have done so
I would be making again a mistake

Confession

Today I want to confess something
Which no one will believe
It's quite strange I think
And will throw the things up my sleeve

I have never said it to anyone
I think people will say I am lying
It's the thing which normally don't happen
The things that I will be saying

Actually, I never fell in love with anyone
Never got infatuated with anyone
The crushes that I have said
Are just to curb the questions of everyone

If I would have said it before
It would be considered stange
It's not that I never wanted to be in relationship
But never got a person in my range

I am so much in love with myself
I am so self-obsessed
That I don't get that feeling
And never have got in that stage

Of course I want to fall in love
I want to make love to someone
But there has to be love which comes from heart
And not from anywhere else

Do I have Friends

Do I have friends?
It is the question that is bothering me
I have a lot of friends maybe
But how many will stay with me

I don't know why I think so
Friends are there for a reason only
Are they to advise me on every matter
Or they are for passing the time only

I am confused about everything
The whole thing bothers me
The friends are there to mock you
Or are they the Pillow where you can cry easily

You share your feelings
Without the feeling of getting it leaked
You believe them blindly
And think that everything is sinked

I wonder do I have such a friend
The friend with whom my secrets are safe
Will you let me a pillow to cry
And forward their own to make me feel safe

I sometimes feel I am lucky to have some
But sometimes everything goes in vain
What is the thing that actually is my concern
Is what bothers me again and again

I have had friends with whom I can enjoy
I have friends who have stood up for me
I have friends whom I do believe
And some who have no faith in me

Choosing friends is a tedious job
Finding friends is easier than you thought
Social networking sites are there to do it
But to have beautiful friends is a very tough task

I have failed or passed in this friendship test
I do not know
Have I conducted this test
I do not know

Please someone help me
In clearing my doubt
Or should I visit a counsellor
In order to clear my doubt

My Love

The emotions are quite surprising
They just come out without expectation
There is a sudden change in it
I am lost in every situation

Your eyes are deeper than the sea
I want to dive in these whole day long
I want to touch its inner Depth
I want to get lost in them so never to be found

The silky hair of yours
The fragrance of your hair
Makes me lose my senses
Leaves me in great despair

Your face I always see everywhere
You are beautiful in every case
Your beauty mesmerises me always
Always leaves me speechless

I cannot sense myself
When you are there
I just want to be with you
And hold your hand always

I trust you with all my secrets
I do believe in whatever you say
I can never lie to you
Even if circumstances compels me in any way

I had never felt like this before
The feeling is strange for me
I just want you by my side
And that always surprises me

You have become my life
Now you are my oxygen
You are my painkiller
You are my anti-allergens

Child Within

You may have grown up
Your maturity level is reached
You may be able to be a parent now
Your ideals may have been preached

It's good to act like a child
There is always a child within
It's good to return to your innocence
And discover yourself within

Think like a child
If you want to imagine
You will see a different picture
Altogether you will be in a different scene

Talk like a child
You will sense purity
The words you speak will mean nothing
It will make you stressed free

Ask questions like a child
Be a little inquisitive
It will open up your mind
And make your wisdom increase

Play like a child
As you will learn to forgive easily
The lesson which is to be learnt
And will make you socially wealthy

Eat like a child
As if no one is near you
The food will taste better
Than what it would be for you

Cry like a child
Open up your heart
Let out your emotions
And live happily your part

Complain like a child
As sometimes it's good to blame others
You will feel safe
Like you are in the arms of your father

Scream like a child
Let out all your anxiety
Make it obvious to others
Set back your priority

It's good to be a child
It makes you realise yourself
You are never meant to grow up
But circumstances happen itself

You will be Remembered

It was a well planned move
In every sense
It was the day which had to come
Crossing every fence

I know not what to say
I don't know how to say
I want to thank you for everything
But I don't have a proper way

The things won't be same
Without you
There will always be a gap
Which can only be filled by you

You have made work fun
You have distressed every situation
Your jokes, your sense of humour
Will always be remembered in times to come

The way you flirted
The way you said everything
There was always some laugh
Reserved for every word spoken

You have been tall
Taller than anyone else
The words you spoke
Have given you a place higher than anyone else

Whenever I will joke
You will be remembered
Whenever I will see lunch
You will be remembered

The moment we have shared
Will always be cherished by me
When you achieve something big
I hope you will not forget me

Rain Dance

Rain is so beautiful
I hope you were there with me
The scene of Bollywood
Is to be made real by me

I want to dance with you
Get wet in your arms
I want to do the rain dance
And lift you up in my arms

We will dance in the rain
Till we are totally wet
The whole world sees our performance
And it looks like a movie set

We get so close
That we can hear our breath
Dancing we forget everything
And the love is poured out of us

Fate and Luck

Luck is the name to curse
Fate is the horrid image
Life can be made or destroyed
By these two types of sage

You may have a dream
You may be in the verge of achieving it
It's the luck which may do a tale-spin
And get you stuck in the middle of it

Destiny is what to be achieved
You may not be able to see the path
The luck may make your work easy
Fate will show you the path

You have dreamt of the kingdom
That is made up of your hard work
You are lucky enough to get it
But wind of fate may shatter it with no effort

The whole world may be with you once
May come to resort you
But when time changes
They will not even look at you

Good fate comes with good luck
If both are there you achieve everything
If you happen to have one, you may achieve
But when none are there you have nothing

It's in your hand to change your fate
Luck me not be with you
But hard work actually rules it
So work hard, fate will be with you

Mother- a precious gift

Mother is anyone's most precious gift
There is no substitute for her
She is the first friend in one's life
You are introduced to the whole world by her

She sacrifices every bit of her life
To make the life of a children
Before every bite she takes
She thinks of the food eaten by her children

When you are not feeling well
She was spending the Sleepless Night
She was taking care of you every time
And giving you the courage to win the fight

When you are in danger or in pain
You will call her name at every age
You only remember one name to be called
But you can't take her name to praise

When you want to cry
You only find one place to hide
You shower your eyes in front of her
You take refuse to her lap this time

When you want a solution to your problem
When you want help in some way
You take no time in calling her
As you know she will always help you in any way

Your mother is your first teacher
She teaches you everything
When it's time for you to take care of her
She becomes for you just like a thing

Dreams

There is always a good time
The fate will shine once
Your fate may not be with you today
But it will be there once

It's not that you have lost every time
You will keep on your defeat
One day will come when you will be victorious
And everyone will be under your feet

The things changed so does the time
You will get what you wanted
You need to wait for it
The time will come when you get it hunted

You need to have patience
You need to face every situation
You need to think practically
And handle all the situations

The life goes on so does your dream
Always dream big and fulfil it
There will be a lot of ups and downs
You are not allowed to be kept trapped in it

Dreams are a part and parcel of life
Life is nothing without it
To fulfil your dreams is not easy
You need hard work and dedication in it

So dream my friend
Dream may not come true first
You need not get disheartened with it
You need to carry on your thrust

Responsibility

Responsibility is a great teacher
It teaches you the meaning of true life
It is a very strict teacher indeed
And makes you reach the thrive

It gives you the opportunity
To learn from your mistakes
It teaches you to stand up again
It makes your life never at stake

I know it's a cruel teacher
It never gives second Chance
It's like a goldsmith strike
Strike you at every glance

It's a perfectionist in every aspect
It makes you a perfect gentleman
It makes you step in someone's shoes
It guides you every time

It teaches you not to give up
There is a different possible way
All the things can be done
In one or another way

Responsibility doesn't come by age
It comes without a say
When you think you are not ready for it
Is already waiting in your way

Letter to Mom

I remain silent now days
Though there is a lot to say
Please do not think I am ignoring you
But my sorrow should not be in your way

Grief can't be always said
It is very personal, deep inside
My worries are burdening me
It is cutting me, making bruises inside

I have no one whom I can say these things
These are too emotional indeed
I have no choice other than to keep it
Deep inside my heart indeed

People will never believe it
They may even laugh at it
But even if they believe it
They will never believe the cause of it

This may be my side of the story
There is always a flip side
The other part I don't know
So it's better to keep quiet

I have to do something
To get rid of it
The grief is too personal
That I cannot tell it

I miss you mom
And will always do
I have the responsibility that you gave me
I am doing it without the will to do so

I will one day run away from it
So I ask you to forgive me
I hope you will forgive me
As this is now eating me

I know you know my pain mom
But now you can never do anything
Hats of to you mom
How you did for us everything

Before I could show my love to you
You are so far that now my words don't reach you
I hope you feel what I feel
I wish I could say that I always have loved you

Truth

Truth is always bitter
No one can in anyway handle it
It comes to you in weirdest of moments
No matter how much you run from it

I think we should be open minded
That is the problem we are facing
In that case whatever comes is accepted by you
You will find the solution of problem we are facing

It is difficult to face the truth
It is never sugar coated
Once the truth reveals itself
It gives satisfaction as intended

Truth can never be easily accepted
It is very harsh and cruel indeed
Lies how much ever good it may seem
Is to deceive you in every deed

lies are delicious and looks good
They are like the Diwali sweets
Truth is like the bitter gourd
It has a lot of true benefits

You have to be strong to accept it
You have to be clever not to ignore it
You have to find ways to digest it
It is the best way to get stronger indeed

Superstition

Superstitions are the things
Which we all believe in
They are not what you may know why
But as it has been there so we believe in

A black cat crossing your road
A glass of milk spilt on the floor
The unlighting of the holy lamp
Are all believed to be ones to arrive at your door

The dream that we see just before waking up
Are believed to be fortune teller
Then the things which I have dreamt at that time
Why didn't come true in the future

I once believed in them
I once thought that they were true
But as time passed by
You come to know they are not true

Sometimes you should try it out
Do what is asked from you
But if it's against your health
You need to take proper steps to stop you

The superstitious remedy doesn't give a totle guaranty
Neither do the evil which is to happen
So why to believe in such thing
When they cannot stop the omen to happen

Why are we so easily moved
We are educated not to believe in superstitions
Then what makes us believe in them
Maybe some came true in the life of a person

People say that the one who believes in God
Believes in superstition
I do believe in the extreme power that is the Lord
But not on the things that lighten the situation

Asking God for help is one thing
But believing that he will help is another
It is rightly said "God helps those who help themselves"
And so you need to work and achieve it dear

If you don't work for your Goals
Do you think you will achieve it?
If you just think that praying will help you
Then you are making a fool out of it